Waterways

poems by

Lisa Kemmerer

Finishing Line Press
Georgetown, Kentucky

Waterways

For my mother, Ruthli Frieda Kemmerer, who loved and encouraged adventure, and also for my swamp-loving siblings, Ed and Jan Kemmerer

ACKNOWLEDGMENTS

"Pantanal Piranha" as "Piranha Fishing." On request at *Fish Feel*. Oct. 2015.
<https://fishfeel.org/resources/arts/#tab-1-12>.
"Entropy." *Stone's Throw*. 2008
"Annelida" as "Tender Annelida" in *Curly Tails and Cloven Hooves*

Thank you to Cara Chamberlain, Bernie Quetchenbach, Jo Houser, Glenda Martin, and the many wonderful people at Finishing Line Press, all of whom helped this chapbook come into being.

Publisher: Leah Huete de Maines

Editor: Christen Kincaid

Cover Art: "Though genuinely good natured, Iris could not keep from
worrying about the diminishing wetlands in her neighborhood"
by Lisa Kemmerer

Author Photo: Jan Kemmerer

Cover Design: Elizabeth Maines McCleavy

Order online: www.finishinglinepress.com
also available on amazon.com

Author inquiries and mail orders:
Finishing Line Press
PO Box 1626
Georgetown, Kentucky 40324
USA

Contents

Barrel-Boat

We struggled up a sizeable slope
    with a timeworn half-barrel
        tottering between bony shoulders,
    enticed by a bewitching
        black bog
    that lived just up the hill.

Plying those gooey-bottom byways
    was a dangerous endeavor,
    our dinghy deficient—
        likely to turn turtle or swamp
        in that unmapped, murky quagmire,
            thick with snapping snakes
            and pop-eyed piranhas.

Our adventure was therefore
    (of necessity)
        covert—
            not to mention that we had pilfered
            that rusted barrel-boat
            from a venerable (yet vulnerable) neighbor,
            who likely wondered by what means
            his chipping tub had traveled
            afar from his tipping trellis.

Stripped to skivvies,
with only cedars to oversee,
  absent time and intent,
we launched our vessel
    to sway, swamp, and resurface,
    all the while marveling at mud-ball malleability
    and viscous bog-bottom suction,

until we sometime thought to dress
    and drift homeward,
        cold and contented.

Chattering through a canopy of leafy limbs
    and across a lumpy sort of lawn,
Mum—forever unflappable
        in the face of bog bliss—
greeted us with a customary
    (and quite convincing)
        command:
        "Clothes off on the porch!"

Bach,

when he sat at the clavichord
feeling out wonderments like *Ave Maria*,
could not have found the necessary notes
if not previously dropped by
      Marsh Wren,
           for example,
trilling tunes over waiting wetlands,
        where Cricket Frog also croons.

Mysteries of the Marsh

Water-winds whispered over the impeccable pond—
    graced with emerald algae,
    ringed with cattails,
    and surrounded by sword ferns, salal bushes,
        and super-sized cedars.

Bony blackbird toes latched tight
    to lush greens that huddled about the edges,
     bobbing with winds
        that harried, whisked, and scoured
            the land.

Frogs croaked (if we were quiet)—
    tucked under the water's
    dark and undulating edges
        in their leathery jackets
    inviting imitation.

Tantalizing tadpoles
    wiggled in and out of the water's murk,
    plump and soft like eyeballs,
        tempting half-size boots
        deeper into mysteries of the marsh—

    a safe-haven for school-weary scamps
        seeking refuge from civilization's
            wearisome ways.

Impressions

Intriguing travelers
scurry between reeds and weeds
along a lightly lapping lake,
scrolling a squelchy score of mudsong.

Winter Tracks

When streams were solid and silent,
we pulled on our layered socks and jumbo gumboots
surged into whitened woods on shaggy ponies,
    chasing bawdy brigands
        and shadowy sasquatches,
    charging over the rocky mountains of Montana,
        down the slippery slopes of Siberia,
        and across the Arctic's untouched tundra.
We paused only briefly
    to examine the complex of bejeweled pathways
        crisscrossing the snow's crust, surprised that

someway,
    our tricky trail of slush
        always circled back
    from far flung adventures
        to a familiar batch of trees
            not far from the barn.

Summer Hunt

When the lake was swimming-warm
    and morning chores a memory,
we rushed from our shabby but shiny home
    on half sized horsebacks (not quite shed of winter hair)
in search of brontosaurus bones and snow leopard leavings—
        finding only pocket-sized pony prints.

Undaunted,
    we turned to the hunt,
sending ski pole spears soaring
    strong and straight
        into soggy stumps and earthen banks
    until twilight turned us tired
        toward our hidden cave,
            wigwam, or backcountry cabin.

Though we clattered and prattled through the door
    with dirt and hair
        stuck to our boney butts,
it was those blotchy feet
    poking from pony print pajamas
    that doomed us
        to a bath before bed.

Earthen Hut

Nestled into rust-colored needles
in the hollow of an old-growth stump
    topped with fir boughs and ferns,
we lingered
      on the mossy margins of imagination,
        lost to easy sleep
    as rains soft-touched the woods,
        waking to a wet and rhythmic tick-drop
          streaming through like sand.

Aurora

Out with the tide,
        in on some distant shore—
you lap at a beam
        of Northern Lights
soon to fade and
        dance on a distant sky.

Gubye

"Six Weeks," I shouted,
peering between dog-nose smudges
on a back-seat window
in an over-stuffed car.

You clomped forward
in Dad's impervious gumboots,
crystal drops gleaming from every nexus
     of our chain-link fence,
waving with both hands—
                    "Gubye!"—

I saw your salutations,
     but your voice was lost to crunching gravel,
and many years from that far-gone farewell,
     I still hold your waving hands—
          though they now carry the weight
               of assumed ease that graced
                    those many comings and goings.

Through nose-graced glass
     on a glistening grey day,
I still hear that silent sound—
     "Gubye!"—
conveyed and accepted
     as if time would not
               trade us
     (and our treasured memories)
          for seemingly endless others,
     just as darkness
          folds that last touch of evenglow
               into untold tomorrows.

Spring Breeze

Passionate pink petals
laced with white grace
    windflutter
into a greasy gutter.

Sweet Together Days

Light feather ways,
pleasant weather haze,
mountain heather plays,
sweet together days—
    all the gone-aways.

Daylight still brings
an abundance of things,
but there's no one to see
or wander with me,
    only two soggy shoes
        in soft morning dews.

I sometimes still go
where moonlight would glow,
to ponder the waves
and bygone days.
    I wonder—

        can there be a fresh start,
        summer cherry tart,
        tender child's heart—
            or is there only torn-apart?

Sunrays say
    of that bygone day:
not the cozy core,
    something else tore,
not our pith and gist—
    that couldn't fail us,
    derail us,
        would never
        heart-impale us.

Can there be a fresh start,
    summer cherry tart,
        tender child's heart,

            or is there only torn-apart?

Ripples

Waves churn between rocky walls
    around a highline lake,
        spilling silt over scuffed sneakers.
I tarry in turbid tranquility,
    lingering in that alpine alcove,
praying for a perceptual hush—
    for some portion of relief
        from present knowings;

        familiar fingers,
            not yet worried by worn-out skin,
            declined being and doing.

            It works for awhile.

But mindful of laundry
    piled outside the pantry
and dog dishes
    empty in the entry,
        I must sometime turn homeward.

            I know—trivial.

But today I see more clearly
how each pint-sized portion
of being and doing
    ripples
like wind across water.

Hackberry Hope

Crimpled leaves cling
    to strapped limbs
        in a slushy rain—

             resisting.

When they, at last, let go,
  returned remnants
    feed the fray:
      flowering to fade,
      fading to fall
      falling to rise—
        crimpled and clinging
        again to green.

Prelude

Thunderous clap
greets the lifting
of the curtain
of spring.

Me Bucket

This colossal cavern
    of mishap,
      deep and dark as the bottom of the sea—
        personally produced—
certainly seems something of an accomplishment,
    and though currently
      empty as a bird's nest in November,
      my incomparable cavity
        could prove useful:
This monumental cistern,
        it seems to me,
      could hold life-liquids for legions
      of sipping lips,
      or cleansing fluids
        for billions of bathers.

So, from the center of my grandiose grotto,
    I await the inevitable downpour
      with a measure of pleasure.

Entropy

Gusty wind-gone hope,
trust brittle as beargrass,
thoughts muddled with surging waters
    that tumble twigs, leaves, and bits of bark
        seaward on this moonless night.

Later, looking from the kitchen window,
    I remember how bluster
        and windward water
    so seamlessly washed swollen wounds
        and walked me homeward whole.

August Prairie

I caught a whiff of water-waders—
humid hide, bawdy breath,
fermented seed of desert weed—
    four friends
on the fringe of Culter Creek,
        cooling their clovens.

Thicker than Water

Platelets and cells
course thick and warm
through tiny tunnels
that wend and weave
    through wombat
        and yellow-wattled bulbul,
    bluefish
        and black angus,

           reminding that
              blood binds.

Myriad Montage

It is rash to risk, rend, or ruin
  one sliver of this myriad montage,
to mar a meadow metropolis,
    drain a drip of water-slog bog,
     or mute a wee whistle
      (whether from whippoorwill or windblown willow)—
     or even some waiting-to-whistle,
       still safe-harbored in a speckled hold,
        frail as a jingle shell,
         fleeting as *Homo horribili*s.

Pantanal Piranha

In a bluish boat on a brown river,
visitors in bright blouses and khaki shorts
peer through bulky binoculars,
    pointing at purple plumes
    and knobby orange knees
then steer to wider waters
    where they dangle rattan rods
        rigged with beguiling barbs.

A fierce pull hoists a frightened fish
    (notorious for tearing teeth),
who has snatched a death-catch
    that slips between incisors
        and out through an eye.

Gasps and squeals of surprise and delight
    supplant the gentle lapping of liquid
        as I turn my back,
wondering why we are so willfully unaware
    of what is blatantly clear
        in a fish's eye.

Life-hush

Robbed of clinkeling cockles and katydid chorus,
pilfered pich pines and paddlefish,
fleeced of waterlilies and wombats,
the future feels of colossal quiet,

    vastiness of void—

      life-hush,

        glory gone.

Annelida

Frosty fingers snatch another
    (and another)
soft-bodied somebody
    from a water-covered walkway.

Passersby
    pretend not to see.

Boneless beings
    have no eyes,
        no flippers,
            no fins,
and anyone who would leave them
    in those lingering liquids
        (legless and limp)
is certainly more spineless and unseeing
    than a lovely wee worm.

Forgotten Fishes

What did the river-fish think—
trapped in paltry pools
    as the irrigation ditch drained,
defenseless when coons came
    to nibble their nubbed noses?

What did frightened fishes think—
pulled from those puny and putrid ponds,
plopped into colorful but cramped canisters,
    and rattled over a rough roadway to the river?

What did flurried fishes think—
tipped back into flowing waters,
stunned and still as they turned to face the flow,
seizing that singular second
    to shoot back into the life-strong stream?

What did left-behind fishes think—
    their liquid lifeline
        slowly sinking
            into sand?

And what I really want to know is,
    why don't more people wonder
        what the fishes think?

Delighting in Difference

Transparent beach blob
    with looped and lovely violet innards,
        lacy brim,
            and a surround of stinging red straggles—

    a perplexing person,
        utterly bereft of bone.

Swaggering Salamander

Dressed in colors of caution,
    Tiger Salamander
surged over the rough roadway
    with such certainty—
tacky toes pushing pavement
    with tail-powered torque,
        wrinkling with each wiggly weave.

I hastened to hoist that fine amphibian,
    holding her between tentative tips
while her rubbery limbs
    perpetually paddled.
She looked back at me
    with shiny brown spheres
        that bulged like May buds—
    lenses located for wary-watch
        when submerged
            (legs lax and
                long tail trailing).

I took her to the perimeter
    of a picturesque pond
and tucked that tiny traveler
    under a fallen leaf
        for careful keeping,
all the while pondering
    what her peepers might perceive
        and why our paths had crossed.

In time—
    given how busy she was with being
        and the wrongness of roads
            (and *ever* so much more)—
        I came to see that I had passed by
            only for her.

RiverDream

Something beyond the bounded brain
    flows through this wondrous waterway—
what moves midnight calm,
    dashing dawn with moon-bright rain?

Riddles roll over frothy rivulets,
    cavort through crimson clover,
        and twine between scrub willows
            with fronds of eloquence.

Subtleties lurk in lush lichen,
    scuttle under bearberry bushes,
        and roll over water-smooth stones
            teaching impermanence.

Enigma hides under busy byways,
    hums through hushed canyons,
        and flies on ephemeral froths
            that tell much of time.

This hinterland holds all that is holy—
    what moves midnight calm,
        dashing dawn with moon-bright rain?

Noatak

Foot-cold midnight,
Arctic sun,
and two tiny
    paddlers
plying murky waters—
    wearing away walls.

Mosquitoes swarm,
    dense as dawn fog,
        falcon floats
            from a shadowy shelf,
        fox hunts
            between bent boughs,
        and tern pumps
    over frigid shores
where water-worn rocks
harbor her frail fledglings.

Backlit by midnight light,
    brown bear swims the Noatak,
        steps ashore,
            shakes,
    and wonders us
with woolly ears.

I wonder, too.

Looking back,
as if through swags
    of bug mesh—

nothing
    seems so real
    as that
            cold
                in my
                    feet.

Over the Prow

Not far from a piece
    of plastic paddle,
weightless
    amid kelp and cockles,
an odd remnant lazily wheels
    before bulging eyes
that bear unblinking witness
       to a deep secret—
          briny burial,
undiscovered deliverance.

Nitty-Ditty Bead

Murky as the mortal mind,
    gritty as grub at the beach,
winded waters surge like certainty,
    rolling rough rubble
        into rounded rock,
    crumbling cliffs
        to scattered sands.

Seas turn easy with the ages,
    quiet as butterfly wings,
        rising and falling in a single sigh,
            all the while housing
a host of unrivaled happenings—
    blowholes breathing and bivalves filtering,
    phytoplankton busy with photosynthesis,
    and filmy fins perpetually pulling
        by way of propelling.

        This bit of black ink
            on bleached white
        holds but a nitty-ditty bead
            of that briny bounty.

Sculpture

Rounded remains of redwood,
    pastel pieces of coral and clamshell,
      shards of shale and siltstone
    pitched and ground to polish—
      the grace of a good scouring.

Sermon

When winter winds beckoned
    on that stark winter sabbath,
I walked unwittingly to the beach,
    where I witnessed
    (with much wonder)
the wreckage of a brutal brine
    flinging lackluster and luminescent sea-life ashore—
        scarlet sea-stars and flaccid jellies,
        crumpled crabs and cracked bivalves—
            still pulsing with presence
        even as they sprawled
                on their gritty grave.

That day's billowing bluster
    also left a beheaded babe
    (lodged in a tepid tide-pool)
        to putrefy,
    partial appendages tidily tucked
    over a mottled middle

        forever muted.

    Why was this decapitated tot
        left to rot?

        Why all of this watery wastage?

    If her flappers had a bit of flip,
        could I so graciously grant her going—
    as I did that flood of smaller
        fishy fatalities?

        Could you?

Perhaps what I found morose and macabre
    (in desperate need of prompt
        and practical improvement—
            if I but could),

only tells of trifling trust—
    insufficient insight.

        Perhaps.

But I was the complete congregation
when the sea spoke of flesh and finality
on that marvelous and malodorous beach,

      and I do *not* believe.

Sequel

How do you feel,
    now that a wave has left you
        to liquefy
    in this sandy cemetery?

Do you quietly covet
    the precious possibility
        of a water-worthy body—
        of washing away
            with a Great Wave—

        a wondrous sort of sequel,

      once again adrift,
        now (and forever)

            on the High seas?

Stranded Sardine

Such a bountiful beach
    with so many marvels—
but only one looked back
    through glorious though glazed
        gold and ebony portholes,
    a singularly lovely citizen of the sea,
        so silvery, silent,
            and still.

I lifted her tenderly.

She was slender, lithe,
    and limp—
her cold scales glistened
    with greens, steely blues,
    and a bit of blossom pink.

It was then that she fluttered faintly against my fingers.

Startled (by hope)
    I rushed to pitch her seaward.

She flew far,
    hitting the hollow of a curved (and compelling) wave,
        and was turned in the tide.
    But just then,
        I saw her slight and shining scales
            shimmer in the sunlight
                as she flipped her fins
                    and surged
        into that swirling sea of possibilities.

Professor emeritus **Dr. Lisa Kemmerer** is an activist scholar and activist artist, internationally known for her intersectional approach to ethics. Kemmerer founded and directs the educational, information-sharing non-profit, Tapestry (tapestryofpeace.org), best known for her Animals and Religion Website (animalsandreligion. org), with accompanying books, and her most recent book, *AMORE: Vegan Ethics*. Working across the disciplines of anymal (non-human animal) ethics, feminism, ecofeminism, environmental ethics, and religions, Kemmerer has written more than a dozen books has been invited to write many chapters for anthologies. She has also written more than 100 articles, most all of which are available on her website or at ResearchGate. In the arts, Kemmerer specializes in anymal portraits, and has created three poetry chapbooks with Finishing Line Press. For more information, please visit lisakemmerer.com and tapestryofpeace.org.

www.ingramcontent.com/pod-product-compliance
Lightning Source LLC
Chambersburg PA
CBHW020222090426
42734CB00008B/1183